Better than Imagined

Better than Imagined

For Those Who Wonder About God

LYLE B. POINTER

WIPF & STOCK · Eugene, Oregon

Wipf and Stock Publishers
199 W 8th Ave, Suite 3
Eugene, OR 97401

Better than Imagined
For Those Who Wonder about God
By Pointer, Lyle B.

ISBN 13: 978-1-62032-877-4
Publication date 1/15/2012
Previously published by Beacon Press, 1999

Contents

One Wednesday night in Renton, Washington, at age five, I was playing around the pews in our local church. My mother was trying to keep me quiet while men and women in the church were praying at the altar. Suddenly I stopped my playing and walked tentatively to my mother. "Could I go pray with Daddy?"

"Sure," she urged. "Just walk up there and kneel beside your dad."

I hesitated.

"It will be all right. Go ahead."

I hesitated—and then resumed playing.

More was going on than my mother knew. Behind the simple request to pray with my dad was a deep longing, an inner compulsion. For me, that moment was the beginning of a lifetime relationship with God. It marked my initial awareness that God deals with people, and He had just spoken to me.

Sometime later, I came running into our home from the yard where I was playing. For no apparent reason, I was crying. I hurried to the kitchen, where I threw my arms around my mother's legs. "Mommy, I feel bad," I cried. "Would you pray and ask Jesus to make me feel good?" There, beside a chair and a kitchen stool, my mother prayed for me, and I accepted Jesus Christ into my life.

Into that stubborn, strong-willed little boy, God placed the desire to please. My dad and mom say it was a life-changing moment. The change was preceded by two promptings of God—one in the church pews and another in the yard of our rural home.

God Initiates Contact with Us

I have discovered after years of talking with people that my experience is not rare. God deals with people of all ages. He may use different methods, but His contact with us invariably affects us.

In the thousands of interviews I have had with people, only a handful say they have never sensed God dealing with them. I have wondered if their experience and conclusion, that God had never dealt with them, was not like Evelyn's. Years before I had pastored Evelyn's sisters in another state. Upon hearing that my former parishioners' sister had been placed in a nursing home close to the church I presently pastored, I drove there to meet her for the first time. Evelyn was a genteel and pleasant conversationalist. After a few minutes she said something that startled me: "I think I am losing my mind. I guess it is not uncommon when people enter a nursing home for that to happen," she concluded.

"What are you feeling? What makes you think you are losing your mind?" I asked.

"I am feeling anxious," Evelyn confided. "I am recalling episodes from my life that I have not thought about for decades. They are very troubling, and I think I am becoming obsessed with them."

Sensing what she might be experiencing, I inquired gently, "Are you comfortable telling me about any of those memories?"

"I think I can tell you." Her eyes stared momentarily at the carpet, then moved to one side; and with a slight catch in her voice, she said, "They are not pleasant memories. I guess you could say . . . they are regrets."

"Are you remembering things you wish you hadn't done?"

She swallowed, kept her eyes to the floor, and nodded while looking up just briefly.

"Evelyn, I think I know what you are experiencing," I said. "And you are not losing your mind. What you are experiencing is what in the church we call conviction. Some people think conviction is negative, but it is just the opposite. Conviction is God working through our memories and our hearts to call us back to Him. Through conscience, He reminds us of what is right. I think He is telling you He wants to have a loving and close relationship with you. He wants to forgive your sins. He wants to take away the guilt you feel for them."

Evelyn discovered that what she was thinking and feeling was really the work of God. Indescribable relief crossed her countenance. She was not losing her mind. That afternoon Evelyn found freedom from her past.

Many people today need to know how God works so they can respond to His love and concern. Before we consider how God works, let's think about what He is like. For what God is like gives rise to what He does.

When Jesus came to earth, He reenvisioned God for us. One example comes from Luke 15, verses 1-7. The religious leaders regarded Jesus with scorn. With condemnation and ridicule aimed at undermining His credibility and ministry, they said, "This man welcomes sinners and eats with them" (v. 2). Jesus, not wanting them to misunderstand what God was like, launched into the story of the lost sheep. The focus of the parable, however, is not on the lost sheep, but on the searching Shepherd. Jesus explains how the Shepherd counts His band of 100 sheep, only to discover 99 are present, but one is missing. Leaving the 99, the Shepherd searches tirelessly for the one lost sheep. We can imagine this Shepherd checking out valleys, wooded areas, ravines, and thickets. Hour after hour He looks, never pausing to rest.

Jesus uses the story to illustrate how God searches for lost people. Jesus announced that His purpose for coming to earth was "to seek and to save what was lost" (Luke 19:10). God is not passive regarding our welfare. He does not want us wandering away from Him.

If we understand that God goes searching for us, we understand more about Him. But we have an inadequate understanding of God if we think He is content only to search. He is a God who searches until He finds. Most of us look hard for something we've lost, but eventually we give up. God is only content when He has found the person who has wandered away from Him.

What happens next in Jesus' story is also important in our understanding of God. The Shepherd brings the wandering sheep home. When God finds a lost sheep, He brings it home. God is never content with the distance between those He loves and longs for. He joyfully carries us back to the place of security.

Coming home to a loving family is a beautiful picture of God's care and inclusiveness.

The story might well end at this point, except that we would be left with an unsatisfactory picture of God's character. For what happens next speaks importantly to what God is like and how we are cherished.

Jesus says God throws a party. He pictures the Shepherd calling His friends and family together, saying, "Rejoice with me; I have found my lost sheep."

To emphasize the point, Jesus lifts us from the human story to a heavenly meaning: "I tell you that in the same way there will be more rejoicing in heaven over one sinner who repents than over ninety-nine righteous persons who do not need to repent" (Luke 15:7).

A rejoicing, happy God takes delight in finding people who have been wandering. This delightful picture of a searching God is life-changing news. We will not understand the remainder of this booklet if we do not understand what God is like. As you read the remainder of this booklet, picture God smiling. Not only is He determined to find us when we are lost, but also He takes delight in the process of breaking through the barriers we have all too frequently raised against Him.

What God Is Like

My friends Al Truesdale and Bonnie Perry wrote, "Long before we were able to identify God's presence or focus on His deeds, He was active. No one is a stranger to God. Long before we ever move toward Him, God has already moved toward us. Even when we do respond, He makes the response possible."* God's love reaches to every person everywhere. God is not about to let people drift aimlessly through life without hope and help. Although we might be inclined to give up on people, God's love knows no limit this side of coercion in order to reach every person—to whom He is deeply committed.

**A Dangerous Hope: Encountering the God of Grace* (Kansas City: Beacon Hill Press of Kansas City, 1998), 49.

Let us explore some of the ways God touches our lives. You may find your story in the following pages:

Creation Points to the Creator

"Do you think much about God and spiritual things?" I asked Jackie.

"Last month we were out on the Oregon coast," she replied. "As I sat on the cliff watching and listening to the surf pound against the sand and the rocks, I felt God was near to me. The power of the surf reminded me how great He was."

The same experience was echoed by Bill, a fellow who loved to hike to remote mountain lakes and fish for cutthroat trout. "Sitting there on a rock on the edge of that crater lake, I sensed God really close," he said. "I can get close to Him in the mountains."

Creation leaves us wondering about our beginnings. We cannot easily conclude that this complex, rational world simply popped into existence on its own. Many people think it likely a creative and personal mind chose lovingly to bestow the blessing of creation upon us humans. The result is a feeling of awe.

The Bible tells how God created the earth and announced, "It is good." Then He made man and woman. Now we look at creation and say it is good. Then we consider that behind the good creation there may be a good God who is attempting to speak to us.

Inner Impressions

God customarily speaks to us through our thoughts. His voice is not strident or condemning. Often these thoughts do not push for an immediate response. It is as though we read a note we wrote to ourselves. Our thoughts seem to emerge from our consciousness, but God is often at work behind what appears to be our own musings.

Some people are more sensitive to inner impressions than are others. Today I was talking with a lady who is sophisticated and well educated. She had a clear inner impression God was directing her to make an important life decision. She prefaced her unfolding story by saying, "I am not given to this kind of thing often. But I think God is dealing with me."

Sensing her uneasiness, I responded, "I have found God often speaks to people through inner impressions. These cannot be explained away, and they should not be. God deals with us at the points of our openness. If we permit Him to communicate with us in certain ways, He will. It was true at the time the Bible was written, and it is true today."

Hundreds of people have talked to me about clear inward impressions that have come to them. "God spoke to me," they conclude. Few will say they heard an audible voice. But the impression was so convincing they knew that God was truly communicating with them.

Human experience and the Bible teach us that God does work through our thoughts.

God Speaks Through Conscience

A second example of being led by inner impressions is the work of conscience. Conscience can be considered God's call to right living. God has built within the human heart and mind a warning mechanism that serves as an alarm when we do wrong.

Conscience has been popularly depicted as a little cherub sitting on the shoulder of a person, whispering in his or her ear to convince that one to do right. Sometimes the call of conscience can be so compelling that people run from the strength of the warning. Jeffrey explained that his feelings of guilt were so overwhelming he felt compelled to sin more, simply to quiet the inner voice. "My conscience was screaming so loudly I wanted to shut if off," he said. "I found if I continued sinning, the voice became less frequent. I pursued sin with abandon. Then I discovered the voice rarely spoke to me."

"One day it dawned on me," Jeffrey said. "'The voice has not spoken for a long time.' I became mildly concerned. Then more and more concerned. Suddenly, I became aware nothing was slowing my race, my downhill race to hell!"

God Encounters Us Through Worship

Hesitantly, Jeffrey returned to church. After a couple of Sundays we got acquainted. Over a period of time and occasional meetings he began to share his story. The voice of conscience began to frighten him less. The call of God became more acceptable. He began to take small steps of faith in compliance with the inner voice. He became comforted by the knowledge that the inner voice was the voice of the Father calling, calling . . .

Jeffrey met God in the church worship service. Tens of thousands of people have had similar experiences. Some of have been overcome in cathedrals, where the austere presence of God seemed overwhelming. Others have found God in the warmth of a relaxed Bible study with friends. Again and again when Christians have gathered together to worship God, He has spoken to those who needed to be near Him.

God Uses People

Throughout history, God has used influential spiritual leaders to minister to people. These leaders walk close to God and become role models for us. They may or may not occupy a position such as pastor or priest. God works through common and uncommon persons. Always, these leaders have been shaped by God, often through great tragedy. As we observe them, we are drawn to the God they trust. We sense He has been shaping them as a potter does clay.

Today there is an accumulating resistance to the influence of Christians. Some people are inclined to lump all Christians together, calling them fanatics, shysters, and hypocrites. Overgeneralizations are common: God is for weak people; all the church wants is your money; you don't have to attend church to be a Christian; I'm as good as anybody else; who do they think they are?

Sadly, professing Christians have spoken unloving words and done discourteous deeds. No one should defend such behavior. On the other hand, many good and godly people have acted kindly and thoughtfully. God has chosen to use them to draw people to himself. Christ's followers tell how God has changed, encouraged, strengthened, and aided them. They explain honestly how God brought peace, deliverance, balance, and perspective to their lives. They testify to the hope, love, faith, and success He provides.

God has decided centuries ago to talk to people through His followers. Their words have been supported by their actions; they practiced what they preached. As a result, millions of people have seen God change them from selfish sinners to growing and pleasant persons. God speaks to us through people.

God Activates the Subconscious

One summer I was rooming with three men who, like myself, were required to commute some distance to work in a sawmill in the middle of Oregon. There was not only a lot of laughter among us but also serious talk as we spent five days each week away from our homes. While Vern treated me wonderfully and I enjoyed his fellowship, he tended to skirt spiritual matters as they came up in conversation. He did acknowledge some upbringing in the church, but he also realized his sins had taken him away from God.

One day I heard him whistling a tune. "Vern, what song are you whistling?" I inquired.

"I don't know," he responded. I whistled the same tune he had been whistling, but he could not identify it.

"The song is 'What a Friend We Have in Jesus,'" I told him. Half smiling he said, "I did learn that song when I was a boy growing up."

This is another example of how God's Spirit works even in our subconscious. God takes personal history and moves it into the present in order to achieve a future good.

God Arranges Events

We have come to expect God to work through converging circumstances. Here is a story of Milena Eneva, who grew up without religious training, but who also saw the hand of God working through her circumstances. Perhaps you will marvel, as I did, as she explained how God began to repeatedly intervene in her life until she became convinced she should give her heart and life to Jesus.

I was raised in a Communist country by Communist parents. My mother and father were and still are atheists. I grew up with the understanding that there was no God. For the majority of Bulgarians like myself, religion was a tool used by the rich people to suppress the poor. I thought the only people who believed in God were either very old and afraid to die, or too weak to face the realities of life. Although I never went to church, saw a Bible, or celebrated Christmas, I didn't feel the void in my life. I was a pretty decent daughter, behaving according to the norms expected of me.

At 18 I saw the hypocrisy of the people around me, especially my parents. My father was the vice president of a local school run by the Communist party. He and my mom had a very good image outside our family, but inside they quarreled a lot. This made me look at education, good behavior, and even family as something vain. Almost overnight I became a rebellious child. I started hanging around with some heavy metal guys, dressing like them, acting like them, drinking and smoking. My parents reacted strongly, and

I was proclaimed the black sheep of the family, the disgrace for all of them. The more they insisted on my being a nice girl, the more I resisted and turned away. There was a lot of anger, hate, and strong words in those days.

With some hope for better days away from the family, I became a student at Sofia University. I searched to find the same heavy metal company there. Somewhere in the middle of the year I realized this, too, was meaningless.

At that time God started acting. There was a really nice guy in my literature class named Bobby. One day, while we were discussing the romantic poets Wordsworth and Coleridge, he opened a Bible and started comparing the images of the poets with the Bible. I was stunned. I could not believe someone so young, intelligent, and handsome could believe in God. What was wrong with him? Later that semester Bobby started talking about God with one of my friends, Galya. Since I thought highly of my intellectual abilities, I decided that she needed some protection from the religious influence of this guy. So I invited myself to their daily discussions and tried to use all my logic to prove him wrong. The more we argued, the worse I felt. I would win the argument and then go home and cry. I did not know why I felt this way. Meanwhile Bobby seemed so happy and peaceful about his future.

I finally went to Bobby one day and told him, "I don't want to talk with you anymore, because all these conversations make me feel bad." But he looked firmly at me and said, "I am not going to stop, because I know that God's angels and Satan's angels are fighting for your soul, and I won't give up." I did not argue. I was glad somebody would not give up on me and considered me worthy to fight for.

Bulgaria was in a very bad economic condition. It was normal for a truck with humanitarian aid to stop in the street and deliver food to the people around. One day such a truck stopped at the university and started delivering something. When I went to see what they were distributing, I discovered it was not food but some books. I took one. On the top of the cover was written, "New Testament." I remember asking my friend Galya "What is a New Testament?" She said, "Oh, this is the Bible."

"The Bible? I thought that the Bible was some bigger," I said.

"Well, it is. This is the Protestant Bible. We as Orthodox also have the Old Testament. Do not read this book; it may have been changed."

Since I was a rebellious person, the command "Don't do something" just challenged me to do it. I started with Matthew, but the story seemed dull. I went to Mark and discovered the same story. Apparently Luke and John were also the same, so I skipped to Acts, which was also very confusing with all these names. I finally found something I liked—First John, the love letter.

One day I went to Bobby and asked what I thought would be the hardest question to answer. "If there is a God, why did He create us?"

"Well, why would a wife and a husband want to have a child?" he asked. "It is because of their love they create a child. So

God because of His abundance of love made us."

The answer seemed for the first time so logical, it spoke directly to my heart. I guess that was the first time the Holy Spirit told me something, without me knowing it was the Spirit speaking.

I also asked him how one knows God exists. He told me to challenge God. "Ask Him for something not very selfish, but something you would know only God could do."

So one day, when I was completely alone, I knelt next to my bed, made a cross with my right hand, and presented my challenge to the Lord. The request was very pathetic. I had met a handsome man, and I did not know his telephone number or address. So I asked God to have me run into that man on the 15th of May. I thought if I gave God a date, it would be harder to say it was just coincidence. The 15th of May came. I was very anxious to see whether something would happen. I left my apartment, took a bus, rode a few stops, got off, and started walking along a street.

I was almost ready to turn around and go home when a bus passed me and stopped at the corner. Out of that bus came the guy I had prayed for. He looked at me and said, "Hi, what are you doing here?" Well, I couldn't tell him exactly, but he told me he had been in Turkey the last few days doing some business. He had received a note saying things in Bulgaria were not going right, so he had to come back.

I had just met him on his way back home. I was shocked to realize God would go to such trouble only to prove himself to me.

From that day forward I knew there was a God. But Bobby had also told me I needed to believe with my heart, not my head. I did not know how to do that. No matter how I tried, my heart was full of doubt and fear. I started reading the New Testament more, but this did not help. It was still boring.

One day after 15 minutes into the Bible reading, I fell asleep. I had a dream that I know was from God. I dreamed Bobby and I were talking when suddenly somebody put his hands on my head—huge, big hands that covered my eyes, shielding all the light. I was wrapped in complete darkness inside and outside. Suddenly from above came a stream of bright light, with an accompanying sense of indescribable warmth, love, and acceptance. I felt as if somebody was telling me, "Do not be afraid; God loves you." The next moment I woke and knew God was the Source of these sensations. My heart was touched in an incredible way. Suddenly, I had faith.

Later that week, after a long struggle with myself, I made a decision to try this thing called Christianity. I remember threatening God that day, telling Him that if this is as fake as everything else in this world, I would never, ever believe in anything else. I told Him I was giving Him a chance to prove himself. I even pointed a finger toward heaven.

God has not disappointed me. He proved himself more than faithful to everything that was written about Him. I praise Him!

God Designs Order

While converging circumstances can point to God's workings, the colliding of circumstances can leave us with questions. "What about when things do not make sense?" we ask. Behind the question lies the assumption: things should make sense. There is a deep longing within the human heart to explain confusing issues. When injustices occur, we want clarification. This natural desire within the human heart to make sense of the nonsensical illustrates the need for an all-knowing God. When tragedy happens, none of us has ready answers. We recognize some happenings are simply outside of the realm of human influence. Explanations can only be found in suggesting there is a God who lives and brings victory out of sorrow.

God's Goodness Invites Us

Within human experience there is a deep drive or an inner oughtness. For example, people feel they ought to be good. That sense of goodness is placed in the human heart by God. Unfortunately, some misunderstand their personal goodness to be sufficient evidence for their acceptability to God. The sad result is that our own goodness may, in fact, insulate us against Him. We do volunteer work, help the poor, or become involved in church or charitable organizations in an attempt to please God. Fortunate is the person who realizes all of one's good deeds never suffice to please Him, because any measure of sin counterbalances the good we do. Blessed is the person who interprets the inner drive for goodness to be a calling to God, rather than a necessity in order to please Him.

Damon was every bit a gentleman. Although a relatively young man in his 30s, he had developed the courtesy typical of a Southern gentleman. He invariably opened doors for people, greeted them with warmth, and volunteered to help whenever a need was expressed. It was hard to imagine that Damon was not a Christian, because his life was so filled with good deeds, an open spirit, and generous ways.

"I always liked to please people. I hoped the things I did would cause God to smile upon me," Damon said. "I recognized after I had done lots of good things, however, my inner spirit was never satisfied. I never knew for sure how God regarded me."

Although Damon did not have lots of sinful black spots in his past, he told me openly, "I have done things I am too ashamed to admit. I knew I did not deserve God's love and forgiveness. My uneasiness regarding His attitude toward me had driven me to counterbalance my past with an abundance of kind deeds. It was not that I did not care about people; I really did. But I really longed to have God's approval on my life."

The day came when Damon gave his heart to Christ. He confessed his sin to a loving Savior who accepted him and assured him that he belonged to Him.

God Touches Our Emotions

Some people have become angry with God and thought they had a reason not to believe in Him. They chose not to trust Him. Such people usually misunderstand what God is like. They think He has promised that life would be fair and that somehow He would make sure tragedy cloverleafed around them. When the tough times hit, they concluded God is to blame.

Others whose anger had became focused on God recognized they, in fact, had a need for the God toward whom they carried a lot of resentment. Although they became angry with God, they realized He was not disturbed by their anger. He is pleased they would come to Him, often in prayer, with their unfavorable review of His performance. God always prefers we are in conversation with Him, rather than to choose to ignore

Him. Our anger toward God never distances Him from us. He is within earshot to take the verbal abuse we shout at Him. At the same time, He stands ready to give us the peace we do not deserve but desperately long for.

One young businessman rising in management circles told me how he was upset with God. As Matt expressed his emotions, he began to see how unreasonable his feelings were. A human taking God to task! He said, "I put aside my anger long enough to say, 'God, I am talking to You because I have some strong, strong feelings. My conversation with You logically leads me to believe You can somehow make a difference.'" God used this sudden personal and spiritual insight to eventually bring him to Him. Several additional encounters with God prompted Matt to begin to attend church. Only a short time passed before he encountered God in such a way that he knew Christ was living within him.

God Implants Our Longings

God jump-starts a host of inner longings to direct us to Him. Inner longings such as new experiences, the desire to be close to God, to pray, to help, and to serve are easily thought to be merely human impulses. Since these inner longings so often direct people to God, we can reasonably conclude He originates them. New experiences are part of the human longings. We may get tired of the routine. We long to venture out of our comfort zone. God has placed within the human heart this longing to experience spiritual truths. And He alone fills the hunger of the longing heart.

Humans desire a closeness to God. Historically, all civilizations have had some form of worship. Often the deities who were a source of worship were made of stone, wood, or precious metal. Each of these idols were human attempts to bring the divine into human experience. Why would people universally seek God? We need to see that the desire for closeness to God begins with God. He seeds the human heart with the initiative to respond to Him.

Prayer is a natural response to tragedy or difficulty and is humankind calling out for deity. Our inadequacies speak to us of the need for someone greater than us. Though our faith may be small, God has assured us even faith the size of a tiny seed inevitably brings His response.

Another longing of the human heart is to help others. While all of us are selfish and look out for our own best interests, we have a competing desire to be of service to others. Helping people is a God-given response to a God-given longing. The desire to bring happiness, goodness, and love into the lives of other people, even if it inconveniences us, is a gift from God.

God Speaks Through the Bible

Some people have a continuing interest in the Bible. They want to know what God says. Some have started reading the Bible only to be disappointed, because they did not feel they understood what was being said. Too soon they gave up on finding any helpful information or any spiritual insight. After a while their interest in the Bible waned.

My father had been raised in a marginally religious family. Although they rarely attended church, when someone asked, they would claim to be Baptists. At age 21, Dad met a young man who gave him a Bible. At this time Dad was serving as a night watchman. He began to read on his break times at work. On one particular evening he was sitting in the dining hall on top of a table. Suddenly the Bible became clear to him. The clearest message was that God wanted him to draw near to Him. My dad bowed his head and began to pray. God met with him. His life was changed. From that day forward he began to grow in his knowledge and understanding of what God wanted. His lifestyle began to alter in order to come into compliance with God's desires and principles.

God as Seen in Jesus

Thousands of people see God in the life and ministry of Jesus. Jesus intended for us to respond to God in this way, for He insisted, "Anyone who has seen me has seen the Father" (John 14:9).

Jesus' life impresses most of us who read about Him in the Bible. His miracles cause us to marvel at both His love for people and His power to perform amazing acts of healing. His teachings stir our thinking as we try to penetrate His profound truths. His death as an innocent man became the reason we can become right with God. His resurrection from death to life provides hope.

We look at Jesus and admit He must be God, as He said He was, in order to achieve such extraordinary feats. The impact of His life down through the centuries is striking: education was begun, hospitals and welfare were initiated, and civil government and democracy had their genesis in the Christian movement. The Church as God's people continues to serve others in helpful and gracious ways. More than 1 billion adherents advance Christ's principles around the world.

Jesus' life was more than a model. We find life, exhilarating life, in Jesus. A close and personal follower of Jesus wrote, "God has given us eternal life, and this life is in his Son. He who has the Son has life; he who does not have the Son of God does not have life" (1 John 5:11-12).

Encountering God

Perhaps you have identified some moments of meaning and near encounters with God as you read these pages and reviewed your own life. Maybe you can identify with the inner feeling that there must be something more to life than what you possess at this moment.

Would you consider allowing God to have a greater portion of your time and interest and faith? Would you consider making a decision to permit His call upon your life to be the call you will answer?

Allow yourself a few moments to wonder at the greatness and goodness of God, who wants to include you in His personal family. Consider letting Him become a change agent in your life. He wants to alter your life's direction, to assure you of His constant companionship, to give you personal peace, to forgive the sins of your past.

God wants to break through any sense of indifference or self-sufficiency you feel. He will pursue multiple avenues in order to gain your attention and win your allegiance. If you have heard or sensed Him, respond to Him now.

Perhaps this prayer will express some of your heartfelt desires:

> *God, You have faithfully sought me. More than once I sensed Your conviction in my life. I think about You. I now want to experience a new and unfolding relationship with You. I open my heart to You. Thank You for Your love. I accept Christ into my heart—I love You and choose to trust You. In Jesus' name. Amen.*